WALKING CLOSE TO

THE VALE OF BELVOIR

Number Fifty Two in the popular series of walking guides

Contents

It should be noted that three of the walks are the same length at $6^3/_4$ miles. Walk no 9 Jericho Covert is flat but can be very muddy. The surfaces of paths are generally better on walk no 3 Harby Hills, but it does contain a stiff climb. The easiest, although over an undulating route is walk no 8 Cringle Brook.

Walked, Written and Drawn by Clive Brown

Published by Clive Brown
ISBN 978-1-907669-52-1

PLEASE
Take care of the countryside
Your leisure is someone's livelihood

Close gates
Start no fires
Keep away from livestock and animals
Do not stray from marked paths
Take litter home
Do not damage walls, hedgerows or fences
Cross only at stiles or gates
Protect plants, trees and wildlife
Keep dogs on leads
Respect crops, machinery and rural property
Do not contaminate water

Although not essential we recommend good walking boots; during hot weather take something to drink on the way. All walks can easily be negotiated by an averagely fit person. The routes have been recently walked and surveyed, changes can however occur, please follow any signed diversions. Some paths cross fields which are under cultivation. All distances and times are approximate.

The maps give an accurate portrayal of the area, but scale has however been sacrificed in some cases for the sake of clarity and to fit restrictions of page size.

Walking Close To have taken every care in the research and production of this guide but cannot be held responsible for the safety of anyone using them.

During very wet weather, parts of these walks may become impassable through flooding, check before starting out. Stiles and rights of way can get overgrown during the summer; folding secateurs are a useful addition to a walker's rucksack.

Thanks to Angela for help in production of these booklets

Views or comments?
walkingcloseto@yahoo.co.uk

52:/

Walking Close to the Vale of Belvoir

The Vale of Belvoir is dominated by Belvoir Castle, the ancestral home of the Dukes of Rutland. A castle was built on the site soon after the Norman Conquest, this developed into the structure that was badly knocked about in the Wars of the Roses and the Civil War. A 17th century replacement was rebuilt in the romantic style but was destroyed by fire in 1816, the year it was completed. The present building was built in the same impressive design and remains almost unaltered today.

The castle appears regularly as a location in films and historical dramas; parts of 'The Young Victoria', were filmed here. It was also the Castel Gondolfo in the 'Da Vinci Code'.

Belvoir has been owned by the Manners family since it was inherited by George Manners in 1508. His son Thomas was created Earl of Rutland in 1525, their descendant John Manners became the 1st Duke of Rutland in 1703. Perhaps the most famous member of the family was John Manners (1721-1770) eldest son of the 3rd Duke, better known by the courtesy title of the Marquess of Granby as he died before his father and never became Duke. He had been a successful General during the Seven Years War and later had a somewhat chequered career in politics. He is remembered in the numerous 'Marquess of Granby' pubs for his generosity in setting up ex-soldiers in the business.

The 1033ft/315m tall Waltham TV transmitter is actually closer to Stonesby. The aerial was first built in 1966 but fell down later that year, a replacement was completed in 1968.

The last meeting at Croxton Racecourse took place on 2nd April 1914.

The 33 mile long Grantham Canal ran between the River Trent near Nottingham to the centre of Grantham, the rise of 140ft going through 18 locks, although the 20 mile section between Foss Bridge and Muston is entirely level. It was built between 1793 and 1797. The canal was badly affected by the opening of the railway between the two towns in 1850 and sold to the Great Northern Railway in 1861. It was not finally closed until 1936. The Grantham Canal Partnership is a group of enthusiasts working in association with local organisations. In 1969 it began the process of restoring the canal. A major problem will be the replacement of over forty bridges levelled during the 1950s to make road crossings easier.

We feel that it would be difficult to get lost with the instructions and map in this booklet, but recommend carrying an Ordnance Survey map. The walks are on Explorer Map nos. 246, 247 and 260. Landranger coverage at a smaller scale is on map nos 129 and 130. Roads, geographical features and buildings, not on our map but visible from the walk can be easily identified.

1 Winter Beck

7¹/₂ Miles   3¹/₂ Hours

Find a parking space in Bottesford; no toilets, all other facilities.

1 Start from the church; take the path left of the church with the railings to the right to the far corner. Turn left through the kissing gate; walk up the path ahead between fences and cross the road and the railway line.

2 Keep ahead, upslope on the path between hedges, over the summit of Beacon Hill, down and across the farm road. Continue ahead on the left hand field edge over two stiles to a metal gate on the left.

3 Turn right, over the field to the gate at the yellow top marker post. Go through and keep direction through the gates to the marker post at the hedge. Turn left to the narrow gate, go through and follow the left hand field edge, with the hedge to the left up to the far corner. Take the wide farm track to the left, with the hedge to the right up to the marker post at the junction.

4 Turn right, over the concrete bridge and continue along the farm track with the hedge to the left through the boundary. Carry on between fields to the gate in the wide gap. Go through and bear left to a stile in the fence; turn right, passing right of the farm and follow the substantial farm road over the cattle grid. Continue up the slope along Skerry Lane all the way, under the railway and up to the A52.

5 Cross this busy road carefully, turn left along the wide verge to the junction and take the road to the right, into Muston village. Turn left at the church past the gate, along the path right of the church. Step over the stile at the back and bear right, there is normally a path through the grass to the stile/footbridge. Carry on up the path between the houses to the road and turn left, up to the junction.

6 Take the hardcore farm road/byway to the right and follow this track as it winds its way down to the Grantham Canal. Bear right; with the canal to the left, to a marker post, (there is another marker post and a signpost close by).

7 Pass right of this first marker post along the path with Winter Beck to the left, the beck at this point looks more like a dyke) and carry on all the way to the road. Turn right along the road past the house to the signpost on the left.

8 Step over this stile and walk up to the stile on the right, cross over and bear left; keep direction all the way to the A52. Cross this busy road very carefully and go over the stile hidden to the slight left.

Completed on the next Page (Six)

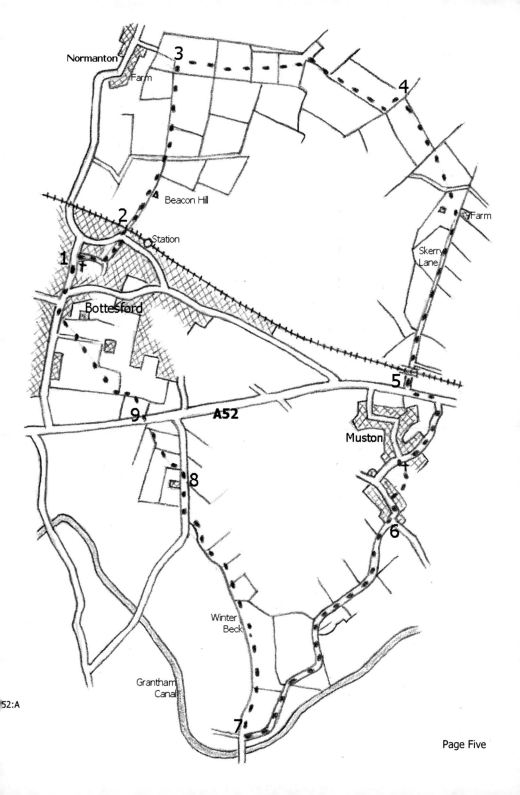

Normanton

Farm

3

4

Beacon Hill

2

Station

1

Bottesford

Farm

Skerry
Lane

5

9

A52

Muston

8

6

Winter
Beck

7

Grantham
Canal

52:A

Completion of **1** **Winter Beck from the previous Page**

9   Bear left, over the two stiles close together and turn left with the hedge and the fence to the left. Continue over the next stile and bear right across a field which may be under cultivation although a path should be well marked within any crop, to the stile left of the church. Cross this double stile, bear left across the corner of a cultivated field and the stile here. Carry on over the driveway and into the playing field. Bear left across the pitch (assuming there is no game on!) and out through the car park to the road. Take the road right, back to the church.

2   Grantham Canal

6 Miles   3 Hours

Find a parking space in Kinoulton village. No toilets. Start from the 'Nevile Arms' pub on the corner of Main Street and Owthorpe Lane.

1   Go down Hall Lane (opposite) and bear right past the cul-de-sac sign; carry on along this tarmac road out of the village. At the signpost as the road ends continue straight on down the grass bridleway under the wires and over the bridge.

2   Bear right and left, follow the dogleg field edge to the gate near the trees; go through and cross the bridge. Keep direction past the double gates and carry on with the fence and the hedge to the right.

3   At the signpost on the right, close to Colston Bassett village, turn sharp right, almost doubling back across the field which may be under cultivation although a path should be well marked within any crop, to the double stile/footbridge. Cross and keep ahead on the wide track on the field edge with the hedge to the left. At the far corner bear left over the double stile/footbridge and carry on with the hedge now right. Keep on the field edge past the stile at the pylon.

4   Bear left over this field and the stile/footbridge; keep ahead with the hedge still right and cross the farm road and the footbridge. Carry on bearing left to the footbridge under the wires. Ignore the first footbridge close to the pylon, cross the next footbridge and keep ahead, through the trees and up the right hand field edge with the hedge to the right. Go through the hedge gap and continue with the hedge now left, to the far corner. Go through this gap and bear right, hedge to the right and follow this farm track left at the corner. Turn right, over the bridge and immediate left; bear right over the midway stile to the road at the far corner.

5   Turn left to the Canal in Hickling Village, take the towpath to the right with the canal to the left and carry on to the bridge in Kinoulton village. Turn right and follow the village street back to the crossroads and the 'Nevile Arms'.

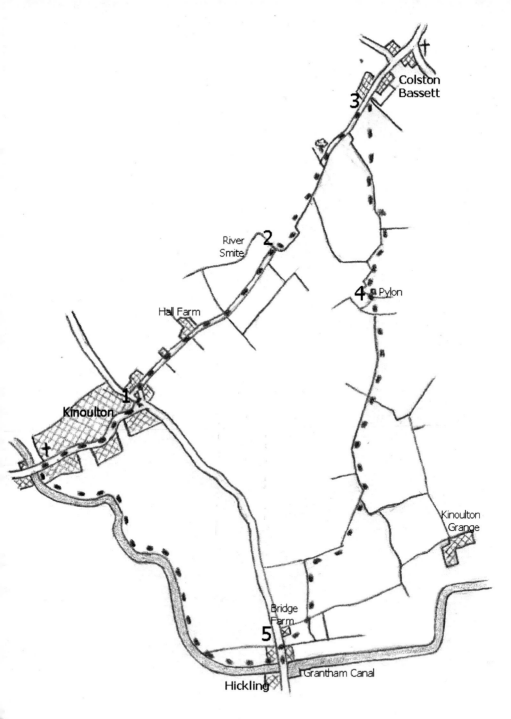

Colston
Bassett

3

River
Smite

2

Hall Farm

4 Pylon

1

Kinoulton

Kinoulton
Grange

Bridge
Farm

5

Hickling

Grantham Canal

52:A

3   Harby Hills

$6^3/_4$ Miles $3^1/_2$ Hours

Use the car park next to the village hall in Harby (at the northern end of the village on the way to Langar). No toilets; small shop/post office and two pubs the 'White Hart' and the 'Nags Head'.

1   Turn right, out of the car park and immediate left along Nether Street; continue across the junction and past both pubs to the signpost on the right. take the path between the hedge and the house and turn left to the yellow topped marker post.

2   Cross the stile, go over the field corner and the next stile, keep direction across the footbridge in the corner and turn right, over the stile in the hedge. Cross the field ahead which may be under cultivation although a path should be well marked through any crop. Keep ahead on the right hand field edge over the stile in the corner and bear left across the marked stile. Follow this right hand field edge and bear left over the stiles at the midway farm road, continue across the field ahead (a track should be visible within any crop) to the marker post.

3   Step over the stile and go up the path between the houses to the road, turn left to the T-junction. Take the roadside path right, with the village of Hose to the right up to the corner and follow the road left, towards Long Clawson.

4   At the next corner turn left along the narrow tarmac road and turn right with this road up the slope and past the farmhouses. Continue downslope between the fence and the hedge to the fork in the road, bear right to the second yellow top post and turn left, passing right of the farm buildings. Follow the track right, along the left hand field edge and bear right through the boundary to the top left corner of the next field.

5   Go through the gap and over the stile on the left, go up the other side of the embankment and step over the stile at the top. Carry on upslope on the right hand field edge with the hedge to the right; cross the stile and keep direction with the hedge still right. Pass through the boundary and bear left then right; exit through the narrow gate at the top and keep ahead between the V of the slopes.

6   Bear right at the top, into the corner and left along the field edge with the hedge to the right all the way to the marker post close to the farm buildings at Hill Top Farm. Turn sharp left across the field, a path should be well marked, to the yellow topped marker post seen against the darker hedge.

7   Descend the slope on the path bearing left through the trees, go through the gate at the bottom and bear slight right to the stile right of the pylon. Step over this stile and keep ahead to the halfway point, bear right, to the gate and cross back over the disused railway line.

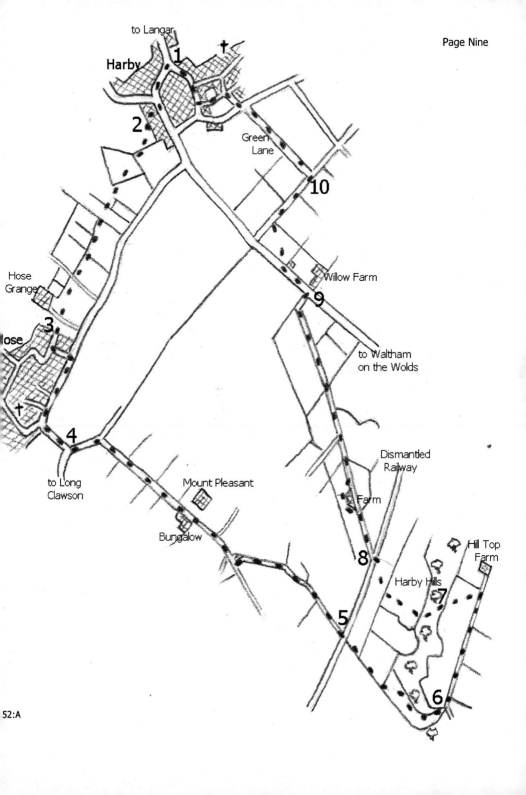

to Langar

Harby

1

2

Green
Lane

10

Hose
Grange

Willow Farm

9

3

ose

to Waltham
on the Wolds

4

to Long
Clawson

Mount Pleasant

Dismantled
Railway

Farm

Bungalow

8

Hill Top
Farm

Harby Hills

7

5

6

52:A

8 Bear right and walk along the field edge, take the path left around the farm and get back to the driveway and the original direction; follow this driveway to the road.

9 Turn left along the wide grass verge for 75yds to the signpost and go over the footbridge and stile into the field. Cross to the opposite corner, go over the stile/ footbridge to the wide green bridleway and turn right down to the junction of tracks.

10 Take this track (Green Lane) to the left, past the houses to the T-junction in Harby. Turn left and immediate right up Greggs Lane, at the top take the path left to the road. Turn left (Burden Lane) and right (School Lane) back to the village hall, the car park and your vehicle.

---

4 Croxton Racecourse

5¹/₂ Miles   2¹/₂ Hours

Find a parking space in Waltham on the Wolds, there is often space on the roadside near the church. No toilets, shop/post office and local pubs 'The Marquis of Granby' and the 'Royal Horseshoes'.

1 Take the High Street away from the A607 towards Stonesby to the signpost where the road swings right. Turn left into Bescaby Lane and almost immediate right, through the narrow blue gate at the signpost. Step over the stile on the immediate left and go up the path between the fence and the hedge. Keep direction over stiles to the hedge gap at the field.

2 Continue straight on across the field which may be under cultivation although a path should be well marked through any crop. Carry on to and ascend the steps ahead, follow the path between the fence and the hedge with the filled in quarry on the left. Continue on the right hand field edge bearing left and bear right and left up to the hedge gap in the corner.

3 Turn right on the field edge and left up to the marker post; take a left hand diagonal over the field (a track should be visible) through the hedge gap and keep direction across this next field into the far left corner. Bear left on the hardcore farm track and right to the yellow top marker post. Go through the hedge gap and continue up the slope of the field (a path should be well marked within any crop). Go through this gap and bear left across the field to the corner of the trees.

4 Bear right along the field edge with Bescaby Oaks to the left, all the way to the second marker post and turn left on the wide track between trees and keep ahead to the byway signpost.

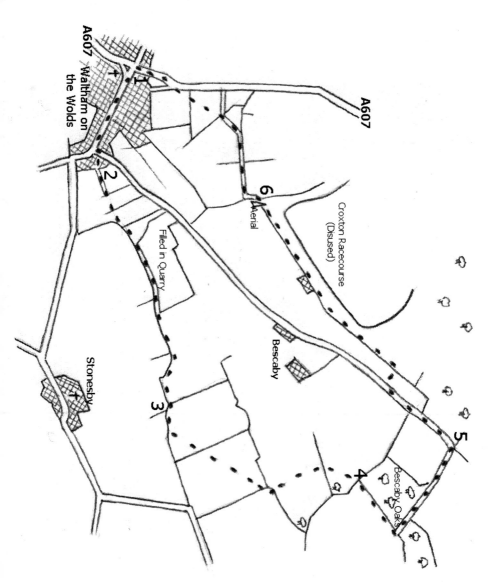

5 Follow this hardcore road to the left, up to the signpost on the right as the trees end. Turn right across the narrow field and pass through the wall gap. Take the track left with the wall left and keep direction with the exercise track and racecourse to the right all the way to the gate at the radio aerial.

6 Bear right and left around the fence and take the tarmac access road to the right. Bear left to the signpost and follow the arrowed direction over the field ahead (a track should be visible), go through the hedge gap and keep ahead to the signpost. Follow the wide grass verge left of the A607 back into Waltham on the Wolds and your vehicle.

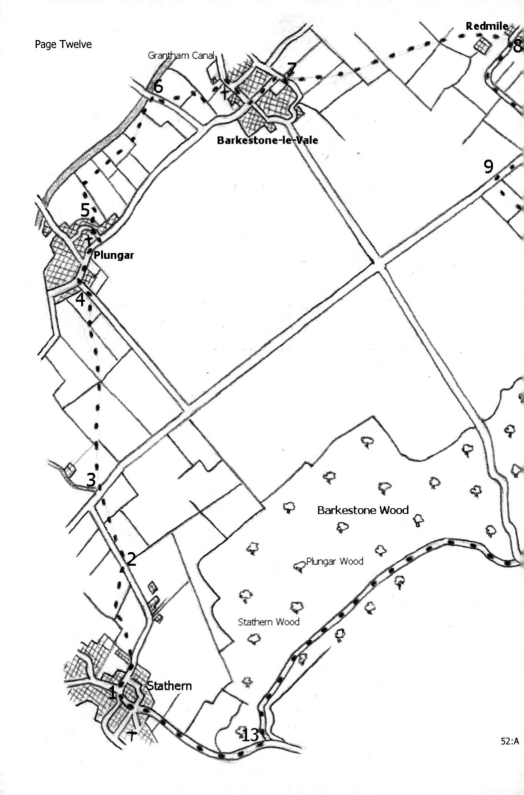

Page Twelve

Grantham Canal

Redmile

8

7

6

Barkestone-le-Vale

9

5

Plungar

4

3

2

Barkestone Wood

Plungar Wood

Stathern Wood

1 Stathern

13

52:A

5   Barkestone Wood

11¹/₄ Miles   5³/₄ Hours

Find a parking space in Stathern. No toilets; shop,
post office, bakers and pubs all in the village.

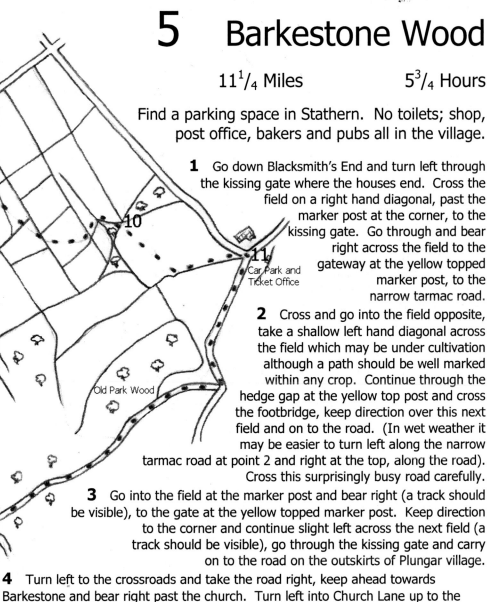

1 Go down Blacksmith's End and turn left through
the kissing gate where the houses end. Cross the
field on a right hand diagonal, past the
marker post at the corner, to the
kissing gate. Go through and bear
right across the field to the
gateway at the yellow topped
marker post, to the
narrow tarmac road.

2 Cross and go into the field opposite,
take a shallow left hand diagonal across
the field which may be under cultivation
although a path should be well marked
within any crop. Continue through the
hedge gap at the yellow top post and cross
the footbridge, keep direction over this next
field and on to the road. (In wet weather it
may be easier to turn left along the narrow
tarmac road at point 2 and right at the top, along the road).
Cross this surprisingly busy road carefully.

3 Go into the field at the marker post and bear right (a track should
be visible), to the gate at the yellow topped marker post. Keep direction
to the corner and continue slight left across the next field (a
track should be visible), go through the kissing gate and carry
on to the road on the outskirts of Plungar village.

4 Turn left to the crossroads and take the road right, keep ahead towards
Barkestone and bear right past the church. Turn left into Church Lane up to the
signpost and turn right (this is a garden), keep right, past the house and go through
the gap at the far right.

5 Bear left through a grassy area past a marker post and continue on the track
along the right hand field edge with the hedge to the right. At the marker post turn
right across the field (a path should be well marked); keep direction and go through
Completed on the next Page (Fourteen)

Completion of **5** Barkestone Wood from the previous Page

the gap in the corner of the third boundary. Bear left down to the bottom left corner and carry on with the Grantham Canal on the left, up to the road.

6 Take the road right, up the slope to the hidden gate and turn left. Bear right, through the gate at the top right, follow the field edge to the marker post and turn left through the gate along the track between fences past the church to the road. Turn right, down to the crossroads in Barkestone and take New Causeway to the left, at the junction turn right, into Fishpond Lane up to the signpost on the left.

7 Step over the stile and take a right hand diagonal over the stile at the marker post. Bear left across this field and cross the stile in the left hand boundary. Keep direction over stiles and past marker posts, through the gateway/bridge at the corner of the sewage works and carry on to the marker post. Turn right, through the gate, keep ahead across the field and over the cattle grid to the road at the edge of Redmile.

8 Take the byway right, through the metal gate and continue to the right, between hedges. Turn left with the track to the marker post and bear left through the gate; turn right, back to the original direction with the dyke to the right and follow this wide track to the road. Turn right along this road for 325yds to the signpost and turn left over the footbridge.

9 Cross the field to the far left corner, go through the wide gateway and go over the field (a track should be visible) to the yellow top post. Keep ahead, step over the stile and bear slight left over a hidden stile; continue direction downslope past the marker post on the boundary. Bear left over this field, through the gate and bear further left across a field which may be under cultivation. Cross the footbridge in the hedge gap and bear right parallel with the telegraph poles.

10 Go through the wide gateway and keep ahead (a track should be well marked), to the signpost and marker post. Bear left up the wide estate road all the way to the signpost at the road junction at the Belvoir Castle entrance.

11 Turn right along the road, signposted Knipton and follow the road left at the corner to the signpost on the next bend. Turn right up the bridleway with the fence to the right and keep on this track with the trees to the right. Go past the cottage and continue to the road.

12 Take the road to the right for 180yds and follow the track left at the signpost. Keep on this path through the trees for a mile and a half to a junction of tracks.

13 Turn right on a more substantial stony track downhill leading all the way back to Stathern, follow the road back to the village centre to find your vehicle.

6 Foss Bridge

$4^1/_2$ Miles $2^1/_4$ Hours

Use the car park at the Grantham Canal between the A46 and
Cropwell Bishop; no toilets, post office/shop and pubs in the village.

1   Cross the disused canal at the road bridge and take the canal towpath north
with the dry canal to the right, carry on all the way to the car park next to the A46.

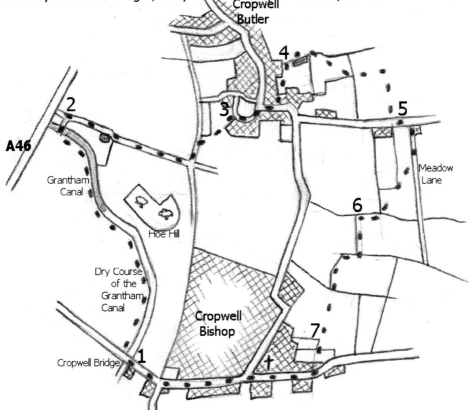

2   Go down to the tarmac \|\| farm track at the edge of the car park. Follow this
track on the hardcore surface away from the road, turn right then left at the large
pond and continue to the signpost in front of the metal barrier. Turn left upslope on
the grass bridleway between hedges to a marker post next to a metal gate on the
right. Turn and take a left hand diagonal across the field which may be under
cultivation although a path should be well marked within any crop.
Completed on the next Page (Sixteen)

Completion of 6 Foss Bridge from the previous Page

3   Carry on passing left of the houses to the road; turn right along the road in Cropwell Butler, bearing left downhill to the junction. Turn right, up to the footpath signpost and left along the driveway to the stile at the back. Bear right over the stile in the wire fence and turn left through the kissing gate to the sports field.

4   Turn right along the path past the pavilion to the stile on the right near the corner. Step over and turn left between the fence and the hedge, as the fence ends cross over to the far corner. The path from here goes straight on from the stile into the field for 300yds to an unmarked point where it turns right to the signpost in the hedge at the road. (It may be easier to follow the field edge to the right and left).

5   Take the road left for 90yds to the signpost on the right and turn right down this wide grass bridleway to the wide gateway on the right. Take a diagonal (a track should be visible within any crop) past the jutting out corner to the bottom right corner. Turn right along the left hand field edge to the wide gap on the left.

6   Turn left along the wide farm track along the field edge with the hedge and the dyke to the right, through the wide gap at the boundary. Follow the farm track right and left at the corner; go through another wide gap at the boundary. Keep ahead over the field (a track should be well marked) to the marker post.

7   Continue with the wire fence and playing field to the right, step over the stile and bear left and right, up the right hand edge of the left hand field over the stile and on to the road. Turn right and keep direction through Cropwell Bishop, past the church and back to the car park on the other side of the village.

7   Windmill Hill

$4^3/_4$ Miles $2^1/_4$ Hours

Find a parking space in Croxton Kerrial; no toilets, local pub the 'Peacock Inn' and shop/post office. Start from the church.

1   Go back towards the village; at the A607 turn right, to the 'Peacock Inn'. Take the turn left into The Nook and go immediate right/straight on, upslope on the farm track between hedges.

2   Keep straight on left of the gate, go through the next gate and continue up the field edge with the hedge to the left. At the top, cut the corner, go past the marker post in the gateway and carry on up the left hand field edge, hedge still left. Go through the narrow gap and carry on to the top of the slope and the yellow top post at the wide hardcore farm track.

3   Turn right down this track, bear left and step over the stile at the marker post. Take the field edge down to the right, trees to the right; towards the bottom cross over the cattle grid and continue downhill with the fence to the left, across the footbridge and over the stile ahead. Keep ahead up the slope of Windmill Hill, through the gate at the top and keep direction to the   stile in the fence ahead.

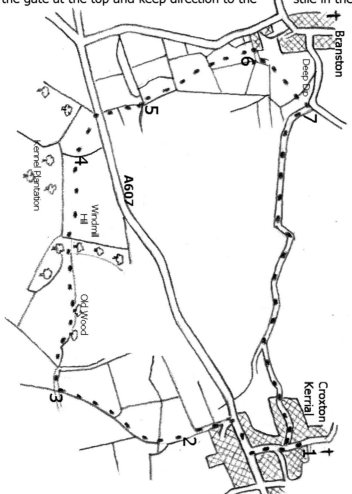

52:A

4   Bear right, across this field which may   be under cultivation although a path should be well marked, to the A607. Cross this busy road carefully and follow the farm track on the left hand field edge ahead. Bear left through the hedge gap at the end and turn immediate right, over the stile.

5   Go down the hill on the right hand field edge with the barbed wire fence to the right, over the stile and the footbridge at the hedge. Bear slight left and step over the stile ahead, keep direction to the stile at the houses of Branston village.
<u>Completed on the next Page (Eighteen)</u>

Completion of **7** Windmill Hill from the previous Page

6 Cross the stile and turn right, follow this wide track to the left and go through the wooden gate to the marker post. Bear right across the field, over the sleeper bridge in the dip and up to the stile at the signpost.

7 Turn right and follow this byway all the way to the road junction in Croxton Kerrial village. Turn left back to the church.

8 Cringle Brook

6³/₄ Miles   3¹/₄ Hours

Find a parking space in Skillington; no toilets, local pubs the 'Blue Horse' and the 'Cross Swords Inn'.

1 Start from the 'Cross Swords Inn'; walk up Church Street to the signpost on the right (hidden at a hedge corner from this direction). Turn right, through the metal gate and go up the left hand field edge, bearing slight right to the stile. Cross and take the path slight left to the far corner (be careful of the hole on the right at the intermediate gateway). Continue from the stile up the left hand field edges with hedges to the left to the double green gate.

2 Turn right along the narrow tarmac road parallel to the telegraph poles. As this road swings right turn left through the hedge gap at the marker post, bear left through another hedge gap marked by a post. Turn right along the field edge and step over the stile and on to the road.

3 Take the road left for 380yds to the signpost on the left and turn left along the tarmac farm driveway. Go past the farm to the marker post on the left and turn right along the wide field edge, with the hedge to the right. Carry on through the wide hedge gap and turn left along the rough tarmac track to the crossroads at the wider concrete road.

4 Bear slight left, over the road and past the signpost; continue ahead on the improved tarmac surface and carry on to the corner of Stoke Pasture, the large wood on the right. Follow the road left down to the corner and turn right, past the front of Mere Barn Farm. Fork left at the marker post and keep ahead past the next marker post along the track between the trees and the hedge.

5 At the signpost on the junction with the byway, The Drift, turn sharp left back to the end of the trees (close to the marker post just passed). Bear right on the concrete perimeter road, right of the low glider hangers (not the main runway) to the signpost at the corner of the trees. Carry on with the trees to the left.